DON'T
WORRY
PRAY

PRIMLAVORA HUMPHRIES

LOVE CLONES

publishing

Love Clones Publishing
www.lcpublishing.net

Printed in the United States of America

First Printing, 2017

ISBN: 978-0692584132

Publishers:
Love Clones Publishing
Dallas, TX 75035
www.lcpublishing.net

ACKNOWLEDGEMENTS

I thank God, that at the beginning of the year, He spoke to my heart, entrusting me to write this book. Throughout the process He's been my strength, confidence, provider and guide. To my husband James, I thank you for your consistent prayers, love and encouragement. You're always cheering me on, I love you my chocolate fudge bar.

To my children James, Sada, Raven and Mason, thank you for supporting me each in your own ways. I love my children and I thank God for you all. My precious granddaughter Brooklyn; your smile alone brightens my day.

To my parents Andrew and Emma thanks for always being there for me, I love you unconditionally. Thank you to my brother Luvell (Karla) for always being in my corner and my mother in law Rosie, I thank you for your prayers. To my in laws, my family, friends and my church family God's All Nation Pentecostal thank you all for your love and support.

I am so grateful for Love Clones Publishing #WeMakeBooksHappen. Lastly, I want to thank Alexica Shelton for the excellent editing of the content of Don't Worry Pray! Finally, I want to thank each and every person that reads the pages written in this book, may God Bless You.

TABLE OF CONTENTS

*If you're going
to worry, don't
pray!*

*If you're going
to pray, don't
worry!*

Philippians 4:6-7 KJV
Be careful for nothing; but in everything by prayer and supplication with thanksgiving let your requests be made known unto God. And the peace of God, which passeth all understanding, shall keep your hearts and minds through Christ Jesus.

Philippians 4:6-7 CEV
Don't worry about anything, but pray about everything. With thankful hearts offer up your prayers and requests to God.
Then, because you belong to Christ Jesus, God will bless you with peace that no one can completely understand. And this peace will control the way you think and feel.

Philippians 4:6 MSG
Don't fret or worry. Instead of worrying, pray. Let petitions and praises shape your worries into prayers, letting God know your concerns. Before you know it, a sense of God's wholeness, everything coming together for good, will come and settle you down. It's wonderful what happens when Christ displace worry at the center of your life.

INTRODUCTION

This book was birthed from a sermon the Lord had given me, "Our God is Greater than your Current Situation". I, myself, am no stranger to life's adversities. During the process of preparing this message, the Lord highlighted to me how much He loves and cares for me, that He will never leave nor forsake me, nor will He ever leave me without hope. I am not to worry, but to pray His Word regarding my concerns.

Don't Worry Pray teaches you how to conquer worrying by praying and confessing the Word of God. As a believer, you serve an all-knowing and powerful God, a God who watches over His own Word to perform it (Jeremiah 1:12). When a king makes a decree or law, even the king cannot change what he decreed. When God speaks, His Word becomes the law by which things are governed. It's imperative to read His word and request wisdom, "and with all thy getting, get understanding" (Proverbs 4:7).

There are believers who struggle with praying. Many have become disheartened and discouraged. All believers have similar concerns and issues that they worry about. Praying and confessing the Word of God are powerful weapons you have to overcome worrying.

that will sustain us to pass the test of faith. Choose to rejoice in the midst of life's difficulties. Put on the garment of praise for the spirit of heaviness (Isaiah 61:3). Say today that you will rejoice and be glad (Psalms 118:24). If you want to overcome your concern, you must not allow yourself to become distracted and bitter by your troubles.

Develop a habit of spending time reading and studying the Word daily. The measurement to which the Word of God is dwelling in your heart will determine the measurement of faith, which will flow in your prayer. By praying and speaking God's Word, it conveys power to stop the enemy because you are using the authority He has given you (Luke 10:19).

I can't stress enough that when you build your prayer life around God's Word, you will surely get a breakthrough. God responds to His Word when we put God in remembrance of His Word (Isaiah 43:46). God moves as we pray in faith. The Word will work in your life as you believe it (Matthew 21:22). Even the angels hearken to the voice of His Word (Psalms 103:20).

Prayer is simply talking to God. It's the foundation of the believer's lifestyle. The effectual fervent prayers of the righteous avail much (James 5:16). The prayers written in this book have scripture references that are easy, yet powerful.

It will aid you with praying and applying the promises of God according to His Word. So as you pray, know that I am standing in agreement with you (Matthew 18:19). Remember, prayer doesn't make prayer work; faith makes prayer work (James 5:15).

Chapter One: Purpose

PURPOSE

Your life does count! God has an amazing purpose for your life. Don't allow anyone to tell you different. Most people struggle daily to figure out their God-given purpose. Even after completing school, having a great career, and starting a family, they still have no clue who they are, feeling lost and empty like there is something missing, desperate for a deeper connection. Before you were even born, God knew you and defined what He wanted for your life. It's all up to you to be willing to live His plan for your life.

You were created in the image of God to worship Him and to have a relationship with Him. Your purpose is a lifestyle of living the way God formed you to live. So seek the Lord to guide you and usher you to fulfill His will that He has designed for your life, and submit to it. When you know who you are in Christ, Satan knows he has no authority over you. God created you intentionally so that you would have dominion, power, authority, creativity, and prosperity in every area of your life.

Scripture

Romans 8:28 KJV
And we know that all things work together for good
to them that love God, to them who are the called
according to His purpose.

Proverbs 3:5-6 KJV
Trust in the Lord with all thine heart; and lean not
unto thine own understanding. In all thy ways
acknowledge Him, and He shall direct thy paths.

Jeremiah 1:5 KJV
Before I formed thee in the belly I knew thee; and
before thou camest forth out of the womb I
sanctified thee, and I ordained thee a prophet unto
the nations.

3 John 1:2 KJV
Beloved, I wish above all things that thou mayest
prosper and be in health, even as thy soul
prospereth.

Genesis 1:27 KJV
So God created man in His own image, in the image
of God created He him; male and female created He
them.

Prayer

Father God, before I was formed in the belly, you knew me, sanctified me, and ordained me. You know the plans you have for me, plans to prosper me and not to harm me, giving me hope and a future, never leaving me nor forsaking me. Faith in God is all I need. Heavenly Father, You created me in Your image, Your likeness, distinguished from all other creation. I am fearfully and wonderfully made.

It's my desire to fulfill the purpose You have for me, using the talents and gifts You blessed me with, for the building of the kingdom of God. Father, I trust You with all my heart, leaning not to my own understanding. In all my ways, I acknowledge You, and You will direct my paths. I thank you, Lord, that above all things, I am prospering, and I am in health, even as my soul is prospering, in the almighty name of Jesus. Amen.

Chapter Two:
Worry and Fear

WORRY AND FEAR

The possible causes of worry and fear are many, which are driven by the works of demonic forces looking for a gateway to plant poison by forming negative thoughts, unbelief, and phobias to gain control of your mind and emotions. That leads to a life filled with hopelessness and torment. The bible doesn't say that you won't ever encounter fear; it says to not let fear rule you. Jesus has conquered the world and Satan. Of whom shall I be afraid? The answer to worry and fear is God's perfect love that casts out fear (I John 4:18).

If you are afraid, it's because you haven't been made perfect in love. Ask God to fill you up with His perfect love and heal you from worry and fear this day. Whenever the spirit of fear tries to return, stop it in its track by meditating on God's perfect love and His Word. Begin to replace worry and fear with love and the Holy things of God (Matthew 12:43-45). Although there are distractions in life, get in your worry-free zone where there is peace.

Scripture

Psalm 56:3 KJV
What time I am afraid, I will trust in thee.

Psalm 34:4 KJV
I sought the Lord, and he heard me, and delivered
me from all my fears.

2 Timothy 1:7 KJV
For God hath not given us the spirit of fear, but of
power, and of love, and of a sound mind.

Hebrews 13:6 KJV
So that we may boldly say, the Lord is my helper,
and I will not fear what man shall do unto me.

Isaiah 41:13 KJV
For I the Lord thy God will hold thy right hand,
saying unto thee, Fear not; I will help thee.

Prayer

Lord, I pray that You help me face the challenges of worry and fear, that You would allow Your peace to overtake my mind, heart, and emotions. I bind and cast out every spirit of worry and fear in the name of Jesus. The Lord is my helper. I rely on Your strength and grace. I will not be afraid. My trust is in the Lord, and He has delivered me from all my fears. My God has not given me the spirit of fear, but of power, love, and a sound mind. And I will keep my mind on the things that are pure and of a good report. Father, I thank You for Your sweet peace, in the all-powerful name of Jesus. Amen.

Chapter Three: Family

FAMILY

The truth of the matter is you have no control over who's in the family you are born into. There are so many families that are torn apart. One of the biggest challenges among family members is getting along because everyone is different and unique. When a member of the family disagrees with you, it's easy to get in a conflict with them. Even when family members don't communicate their opinion in a healthy and respectful way, it can form ongoing problems, which can extend to other family members, causing division and ultimately destroying relationships. Family life today is under siege. It is Satan's passion to keep discord within the family compound.

Satan was rejected and cast out of heaven along with one-third of the fallen angels. He has no father, mother, brothers, or sisters. That ancient serpent called the devil wants to destroy the unity and love among families. God's desire is to restore and save the entire household and to have a relationship with His children. Family was established and instituted by God. When family members commit their lives to Christ and fulfill their role within the family, then peace and harmony will reign in the home and among extended family.

We should strive to build our families upon a solid foundation in the Word of God, adhering to biblical principles, family values, praying together and for one another.

Scripture

Ephesians 4:32 KJV
And be kind one to another, tenderhearted,
forgiving one another, even as God for Christ's sake
hath forgiven you.

1 Timothy 5:8 KJV
But if any provide not for his own, and specially for
those of his own house, he hath denied the faith,
and is worse than an infidel.

Colossians 3:20 KJV
Children, obey your parents in all things: for this is
well pleasing unto the Lord.

Galatians 3:26 KJV
For ye are all the children of God by faith in Christ
Jesus.

Prayer

God, I pray for wisdom to address the issues that surface and resurface in my family, causing dysfunction and disunity during family gatherings and annual reunions. God, I let bitterness and evil speaking be put away. I endeavor to be kind, loving, and forgiving of others, even as God, for Christ's sake, has forgiven me. I will not allow the devil to bring division within my family. No weapon formed against us shall prosper.

God has made a hedge about us. I bind every spirit of selfishness, hatred, and unforgiveness, in Jesus' name. God, I ask that you loose joy, happiness, and laughter that families should experience. Lord, I thank you for restoring unity, love, and forgiveness back into my family unit, in the matchless name of Jesus. Amen.

Chapter Four:
Finance

FINANCE

Poverty is a curse. The spirit of poverty's assignment is to restrict you from living healthy, wealthy, and whole. Its duties are to keep you buried in debt, in ongoing lack, and in an ignorant state. Break and cast out the spirit of poverty from your life, and set your finances free. Renounce all evil acquisition of money. Break the generational curse inherited through your bloodline that was sent to block and hinder prosperity from freely flowing to you. God wants you to owe no man anything, but the debt of love (Roman 13:8).

Once you are exempt from poverty and the mindset of destitution, purpose in your heart to give and sow bountifully and joyfully into the kingdom of God and into the lives of others (2 Corinthians 9:6). Be a good steward over your financial affairs and money management. Live within your means. Pay your obligations on time, and create a realistic budget based on your income. Be obedient and faithful in paying your tithes and giving your offering, that you may plant and produce good fruit unto the Lord, that He will rebuke the devour on your behalf.

Scripture

Malachi 3:11 KJV
And I will rebuke the devourer for your sakes, and
he shall not destroy the fruits of your ground;
neither shall your vine cast her fruit before the time
in the field, saith the Lord of hosts.

Deuteronomy 8:18 KJV
But thou shalt remember the Lord thy God: for it is
He that giveth thee power to get wealth, that he
may establish his covenant which he sware unto thy
fathers, as it is this day.

Matthew 6:33 KJV
But seek ye first the kingdom of God, and His
righteousness; and all these things shall be added
unto you.

Luke 6:38 KJV
Give, and it shall be given unto you; good measure,
pressed down, and shaken together, and running
over, shall men give into your bosom. For with
same measure that ye mete withal it shall be
measured to you again.

Psalm 24:1 KJV
The earth is the Lord's, and the fullness thereof; the
world, and they that dwell therein.

Psalm 115:14 KJV
The Lord shall increase you more and more, you and your children.

Deuteronomy 28:6 KJV
Blessed shalt thou be when thou comest in, and blessed shalt thou be when thou goest out.

Galatians 3:13 KJV
Christ hath redeemed us from the curse of the law, being made a curse for us: for it is written, Cursed is every one that hangeth on a tree.

Prayer

Merciful and forgiving God, the whole earth is Yours, and all that I am and have are Yours. I repent, Lord. Help me to be a good steward over all You have entrusted to me. I break the spirit of poverty, lack, and failure, in Jesus' name. Christ has redeemed me from the curse of the law, and I am blessed in every area of my life. I pray that You give me the blueprint of how to live debt-free, financially owing no man or woman anything, but to love them. Give me a generous heart, sowing and giving bountifully with the spirit of joy and love.

Lord, I seek first Your kingdom and Your righteousness, believing that all my needs will be supplied according to Your promises. It is You who has given me power to get wealth, so that I may establish Your covenant. Father, you are multiplying all my resources. My children and I are increasing, and Your blessings are always more than enough. God, thank You for blessing my going out and my coming in. I am blessed, in the gracious name of Jesus! Amen.

Chapter Five:
Grief

GRIEF

People from all habitats around the world experience loss. Grief is a natural response to loss. It's important to have a positive perspective about grief and sorrow. There is nothing wrong with grieving a loss. Everyone grieves differently. It's okay to comfort one another during periods of grief. When you seek counseling to work through grief, you have the ability to mourn with others.

As a believer, while grieving, turn to God's Word to find comfort and strength. The Lord is near to the brokenhearted and saves the crushed in spirit. God is faithful. In times of bereavement, He is with you. Express yourself to Him, pour out your heart and emotions. He created you, and He understands. He loves you, and He is in control.

Scripture

Galatian 6:2 KJV
Bear ye one another's burdens, and so fulfill the law of Christ.

Psalm 34:18 KJV
The Lord is nigh unto them that are of a broken heart; and saveth such as be of a contrite spirit.

Psalm 147:3 KJV
He healeth the broken in heart, and bindeth up their wounds.

Matthew 5:4 KJV
Blessed are they that mourn: for they shall be comforted.

Matthew 11:28 KJV
Come unto me, all ye that labour and are heavy laden, and I will give you rest.

Psalm 30:5 KJV
For his anger endureth but a moment; in his favor is life: weeping may endure for a night, but joy cometh in the morning.

Prayer

Father, You know the measurement of pain and heartache which I am feeling. But you came to bind the wounds and to heal the brokenhearted and to let the oppressed go free. Father, You said come unto You all that labor and are heavy laden, and You will give me rest. Father, I come to You with grief and all other circumstances that concern me. I cast all my cares upon You for I know You care for me.

Guide me to that place of rest. Pour your peace in my heart. I come against the spirit of guilt and restlessness that seeks to destroy my personal happiness. Weeping may endure for a night, but God's amazing joy comes in the morning. It's morning time!! I receive it, in Jesus' name. Amen.

Chapter Six:
Addiction

ADDICTION

No matter what addiction you are suffering from, it is never too late to cry out to God. Addictions and cravings are sent by the devil to enslave you to depend upon him. With a habit, you are in control of your preferences. But with an addiction, you are not in authority of your choices, which can lead to a path of destruction at home, work, school, and also in your health and relationships. No matter how ashamed, powerless, and hopeless you feel, there is hope, healing, and deliverance in Jesus.

The Word of God empowers, inspires, and strengthens you to conquer any type of addiction, whether it be gambling, drugs, alcohol, self-affliction, pornography, etc. Just like the devil tried to tempt Jesus, he is certainly going to try to tempt you. Say to him that you will not live by bread alone, but by every word that proceeded out the mouth of God. You will only worship the Lord your God, and Him only will you serve.

Scripture

Matthew 26:41 KJV
Watch and pray, that ye enter not into temptation:
the spirit indeed is willing, but the flesh is weak.

John 10:10 KJV
The thief cometh not, but for to steal, and to kill,
and to destroy: I am come that they might have life,
and that they might have it more abundantly.

Matthew 4:4 KJV
But he answered and said, It is written, Man shall
not live by bread alone, but by every word that
proceedeth out of the mouth of God.

Matthew 4:10 KJV
Then saith Jesus unto him, Get thee hence, Satan: for
it is written, Thou shalt worship the Lord thy God,
and him only shalt thou serve.

Prayer

Lord, I pray now, speaking to the soul to be totally delivered from every stronghold of addiction and never to return to it again. Lord, empower me with strength to receive deliverance and begin recovery. I break the power of addiction of every kind over my mind. I trust You for freedom from addiction. I overcome by the Blood of Jesus and the words of my testimony.

I speak that I am free and an overcomer, because I've been washed in the Blood of the Lamb. Lord, I thank You that old things, awful habits, and addictions have passed away, and I now have become new in You. Thank You, Jesus, for delivering and setting me free, in the merciful name of Jesus. Amen.

Chapter Seven: Mental Health

MENTAL HEALTH

There are millions of people suffering from mental illness which affect their thoughts, behavior, and mood, disrupting their ability to perform on a daily basis. This is the work of the devil to enchain you with mental illness, battling of the mind. "For this purpose, the Son of God was made manifested, that He might destroy the works of the devil" (1 John 3:8). The devil desires to keep you captive to psychological and mental abuse. This type of cruelty is not always easy to recognize that it is breaking down your immune system, self-worth, and self-esteem.

Learn the Word of God, and apply it to your life. Use God's Word to put the devil to flight. Jesus came to deliver you from the bondage of the enemy. You no longer have to live with a mental illness diagnosis. God's Word and grace in your life as a believer will renew your mind. You will experience total restoration, mental and emotional wholeness in Jesus Christ, who demonstrated God's power over death and sickness, including mental illness.

Scripture

Philippians 4:8 KJV
Finally, brethren, whatsoever things are true,
whatsoever things are honest, whatsoever things are
just, whatsoever things are pure, whatsoever things
are lovely, whatsoever things are of good report; if
there be any virtue, and if there be any praise, think
on these things.

Ephesians 4:23-24 KJV
And be renewed in the spirit of your mind;
And that ye put on the new man, which after God is
created in righteousness and true holiness.

Isaiah 26:3 KJV
Thou wilt keep him in perfect peace, whose mind is
stayed on thee: because he trusteth in thee.

1 Corinthians 2:16 KJV
For who hath known the mind of the Lord, that he
may instruct him? But we have the mind of Christ.

Prayer

Dear Heavenly Father, I pray grace as one who suffers from mental disease. I apply the Blood of Jesus over negative thoughts that control my thinking. Father, break the power of the demonic stronghold designed and created to destabilize the mind and confuse the intellect. I welcome the Holy Ghost to bring freedom and wholeness to my mind. I declare and decree I have the mind of Christ, and my memory is blessed. Heavenly Father, I thank You that deliverance is the children's bread and that I have the right to enjoy God's best for my life to the fullest, in the blessed name of Jesus. Amen.

Chapter Eight:
Physical Health

PHYSICAL HEALTH

You, like most people, probably read an abundance of material on how to maintain a healthy lifestyle by regularly exercising, eating nutritious meals, and getting enough sleep to build the immune system to avoid becoming sick. But sometimes people are born with physical defects, not because of the decisions of their parents, but because it fulfills the will of God. One example is Jesus healing a man who was blind from birth (John 9). He makes all things new. No matter what you're facing, continue to follow Jesus forward.

Jesus loves you and desires to heal you. He is a God of miracles. Don't believe the lies of the devil and his cohorts about your health and healing. Take control over your thoughts, casting down all negativity that is contrary to the Word of God (2 Corinthians 10:5). Speak to sickness that you are healed, whole, nothing missing, and nothing broken, by the stripes of Jesus. He has given you authority that death and life are in the power of the tongue (Proverbs 18:21).

Continually confess the Word of God over yourself. "God is a healer no matter what my body is telling me and what the doctor report states. I trust God to heal me and bless me with vibrant health."

Scripture

Jeremiah 30:17 KJV
For I will restore health unto thee, and I will heal thee of thy wounds, saith the LORD; because they called thee an Outcast, saying, This is Zion, whom no man seeketh after.

Isaiah 53:5 KJV
But he was wounded for our transgressions, he was bruised for our iniquities: the chastisement of our peace was upon him; and with his stripes we are healed.

James 5:14 KJV
Is any sick among you? Let him call for the elders of the church; and let them pray over him, anointing him with oil in the name of the Lord.

James 4:7 KJV
Submit yourselves therefore to God. Resist the devil, and he will flee from you.

1 Corinthians 9:27 KJV
But I keep under my body, and bring it into subjection: lest that by any means, when I have preached to others, I myself should be a castaway.

Prayer

Father, Your Word says that if there is any sick among you, let him call for the elders, and let them pray, anointing him with oil. And the prayer of faith will save the sick, and the Lord will raise him up. And if he committed any sins, they shall be forgiven. Satan, you have no authority over me. I resist you, so you must flee now! Jehovah- Rapha has taken sickness and disease from the midst of me. Therefore, I command every organ in my body to function as God intended. Any body parts that have been afflicted are made whole, in Jesus' name. You have forgiven all my iniquities and healed all my diseases. By Your stripes, I am healed.

I apply the Blood of Jesus from the crown of my head to the soles of my feet. My body is the temple of the Holy Ghost. I will keep under my body and bring it into subjection, and not allow my flesh to control me. I am dedicated to live a good life, a healthy lifestyle. I confess with my mouth and believe in my heart that I am healed according to the Word of God through Jesus Christ our healer. Amen.

Chapter Nine: Protection

PROTECTION

Many individuals worry about safety and becoming victimized. The enemy wants you to live your life in dismay and awaiting mischief to come among you and your loved ones. The duty of the adversary is to keep your mind far away from God and His promises to you. The Word of God says that He will keep them in perfect peace whose mind is stayed on Him, because they trusted in thee. Focus daily on God, and trust in Him alone, knowing and believing He will shield and protect you and your family from hurt, harm, and accidents, seen and unseen. No wickedness will be allowed to follow you, nor will danger be allowed to come near your home.

Scripture

Psalms 91:10 KJV
There shall no evil befall thee, neither shall any plaque come nigh thy dwelling.

Isaiah 26:3 KJV
Thou wilt keep him in perfect peace, whose mind is stayed on thee: because he trusteth in thee.

Psalm 91:7 KJV
A thousand shall fall at thy side, and ten thousand at thy right hand; but it shall not come nigh thee.

Psalm 91:4 KJV
He shall cover thee with His feathers, and under his wings shall thou trust: his truth shall be thy shield and buckler

Job 1:10 KJV
Hast not thou made an hedge about him, and about his house, and all that he hath on every side? Thou hast blessed the work of his hands, and his substance is increased in the land.

Prayer

Precious Lord, I pray the Spirit of the living God falls fresh. And release Your hedge of protection around me, my family, our homes, and our possessions. I cancel every wicked device that the enemy plans to use. I fear no evil, for You are with me. Lord, You are my defender and protector in the times of trouble, shielding me with the holy angels. Lord, I thank You for covering me and my loved ones with Your feathers. Under Your wings, that's where I find refuge, in the precious name of Jesus. Amen.

Chapter Ten: Violence and Terrorism

VIOLENCE AND TERRORISM

There is a spirit of violence and terrorism in our world, operating through tormented individuals and groups. Believers, be not afraid of those who can kill the body, but cannot kill the soul. Rather, be afraid of the One who can destroy both body and soul. So be not afraid of man. God is in control! Your prayers are not powerless. Go boldly before the Lord, asking that He cast down strongholds and set the captives free. Direct your prayers that the angry individuals and groups that have the spirit of violence and terrorism working through them be free from bondage and the works of the devil. God promises His people a peace that surpasses all understanding. There is safety in Jesus.

Scripture

Matthew 10:28 KJV
And fear not them which kill the body, but are not able to kill the soul: but rather fear him which is able to destroy both soul and body in hell.

Psalm 91:5 KJV
Thou shall not be afraid for the terror by night; nor the arrow that flieth by day.

Psalm 86:14 KJV
O God, the proud are risen against me, and the assemblies of violent men have sought after my soul; and have not set thee before them.

Psalm 91:10-11 KJV
There shall no evil befall thee, neither shall any plaque come nigh thy dwelling.
For he shall give his angels charge over thee, to keep thee in all thy ways.

Isaiah 59:19 KJV
So shall they fear the name of the Lord from the west, and his glory from the rising of the sun. When the enemy shall come in like a flood, the Spirit of the Lord shall lift up a standard against him.

Prayer

I praise the Lord for Your protection and goodness. Lord, I come against every demonic authority that has motivated and controlled the lives of individuals to attack others. I pray that the assemblies of the violent men be revealed and chopped off. I will not be afraid of the terror by night nor the arrow that flies by day. No evil shall befall me or any plague come nigh my dwelling. For the Lord has given His angels charge over me to keep me in all my ways. I will fear not, but stand still and see the salvation of the Lord. For the terrorists I see today, I will see them no more. The Lord is fighting for me. Satan, the Lord rebuke you now! The Blood of Jesus prevails! The adversary is defeated, and I give all glory to God, in Jesus' name. Amen.

Chapter Eleven:
Our Nation

OUR NATION

Our nation needs more than just a National Day of Prayer. God desires you to humble yourself, pray, seek His face, and turn from wickedness. Then will He hear from heaven, forgive your sins, and heal the land. You are to intercede on behalf of those in authority. It is a biblical command you're to obey. Even in the midst of an evil and wicked land, pray without ceasing for God's blessing, grace, mercy, and prosperity for our nation.

Pray especially for rulers and their governments to rule well so you can be quietly about your business of living simply, in humble contemplation. This is the way of your Savior God wants you to live (1 Timothy 2:1-3). All authority has been established by Him to accomplish His purpose, so they might come to the saving knowledge of Jesus. This is good and acceptable in the sight of God, who desires all men to be saved and to come unto the knowledge of the truth (1 Timothy 2:3-4).

Scripture

2 Chronicles 7:14 KJV
If my people, which are called by my name, shall humble themselves, and pray, and seek my face, and turn from their wicked ways; then will I hear from heaven, and will forgive their sin, and will heal their land.

Matthew 13:25 KJV
But while men slept, his enemy came and sowed tares among the wheat, and went his way.

1 John 1:9 KJV
If we confess our sins, he is faithful and just to forgive us our sins, and to cleanse us from all unrighteousness.

Psalm 67: 1 KJV
God be merciful unto us, and bless us; and cause his face to shine upon us; Selah.

1 Thessalonians 5:17 KJV
Pray without ceasing.

1 Timothy 2:1-2 KJV
I exhort therefore, that, first of all, supplications, prayers, intercessions, and giving of thanks, be made for all men;

For kings, and for all that are in authority; that we may lead a quiet and peaceable life in all godliness and honesty.

Prayer

Heavenly Father, in the name of Jesus, I humbly come to you on behalf of this nation. I am repenting of my sins and asking for forgiveness. Lord, I thank You that You are just to forgive my sins and cleanse me of all my unrighteousness. As a nation, I pray we will have no other gods before You. I pray that we will hide Your Word in our hearts that we might not sin against thee. The enemy has sown tares into this nation, and it is time to abolish those tares. I bind and rebuke every terrorist act against my nation, in the name of Jesus.

Lord, I plead the Blood over every candidate and leader serving in office and over those that are in authority, that we may lead a quiet and peaceful life in all godliness and honesty. I ask You to surround them with godly counsel. Father, You see and You care. Lift up the bowed down heads of the people. Give them hope. Let Your peace rule in their hearts. God, be merciful unto our nation. Bless us. Cause Your face to shine upon us, and let Your ways be known upon the earth, in the matchless name of Jesus. Amen.

Chapter Twelve:
Success

SUCCESS

Stay strong and don't give up. Your season is coming. God is working behind the scenes, and you are closer to your breakthrough than you can see or imagine. Define what success means to you. Start setting clear goals, and be realistic. It's important that you see your future and believe in yourself. You're capable of making your dreams a reality. Fight for what you want. Stand for what you want, and never give up on your dreams. Don't put your dreams off because it's hard work, physically and mentally demanding. Just get up and get it done.

Success is a product of your work. You are to work by using your talents to glorify God, to serve the common good, and to advance the kingdom of God. Have faith in God for your success (Mark 11:24). Prepare to show the world how great you are. Do not allow anyone or anything delay your success. When it looks like you've made it, prepare to work even harder.

You are not too old, and it's not too late. You can still make it happen. Walk in your destiny. The enemy will bring fear and try to convince you that your dreams are not worth pursuing, but God is able to give you the desires of your heart and the things that He has for you as well.

Scripture

Philippians 4:13 KJV
I can do all things through Christ which
strengtheneth me.

Romans 8:37 KJV
Nay, in all these things we are more than
conquerors through him that loved us.

1 John 4:4 KJV
Ye are of God, little children, and have overcome
them: because greater is he that is in you, than he
that is in the world.

2 Corinthians 2:14 KJV
Now thanks be unto God, which always causeth us
to triumph in Christ, and maketh manifest the
savour of his knowledge by us in every place.

2 Corinthians 5:7 KJV
For we walk by faith, not by sight.

Prayer

Dear God, Your word says you have given me victory and cause me to triumph through Jesus Christ, our Lord. You made me victorious and more than a conqueror. My life is built upon a rock, and no storm of life will destroy me. I walk and live by faith. I am the seed of Abraham. I am the head and not the tail. I am above and not beneath. And I can do all things through Christ who strengthens me.

During seasons when I want to relinquish my responsibilities, the Spirit of God comes to refresh and give me strength to press through to victory. The greater One lives in me. His favor is with me, in Jesus' name. Amen.

Chapter Thirteen: Salvation

SALVATION

You cannot buy or earn salvation. You are saved by God's grace and your faith in His son, Jesus Christ. Salvation is attained by acknowledging you are a sinner, asking for forgiveness, believing Jesus died for your sins, believing He rose from the dead on the third day, and confessing with your mouth the Lord Jesus. When Jesus died on the cross, He provided salvation for all. He desires to have a close relationship with you, to teach you His ways, and to bless you.

Also, get involved in a local church that preaches the full gospel (Hebrews 10:25). Satan is committed to keeping every individual blinded of the truth about salvation. He knows salvation is totally free. It was paid in full at a great sacrifice by Jesus, through an agonizing death on the cross. Jesus paid the penalty for your sins and removed the barriers that separated you from God. The moment you become born again, God sees Jesus in you, not your sins. Those sins were forgiven and cast away, never to be seen again.

Scripture

John 3:16 KJV
For God so loved the world, that he gave his only begotten Son, that whosoever believeth in him should not perish, but have everlasting life.

Romans 10:13 KJV
For whosoever shall call upon the name of the Lord shall be saved.

John 14:6 KJV
Jesus saith unto him, I am the way, the truth, and the life: no man cometh unto the Father, but by me.

Acts 2:38-39
Then Peter said unto them, Repent, and be baptized every one of you in the name of Jesus Christ for the remission of sins, and ye shall receive the gift of the Holy Ghost.

John 3:3 KJV
Jesus answered and said unto him, Verily, verily, I say unto thee, Except a man be born again, he cannot see the kingdom of God.

Prayer

Lord Jesus, I am calling on Your name. I believe in my heart that you are the Son of God. I thank You for dying for my sins and taking my place. I believe God raised You from the dead. Take control over my life and help me to be the Christian You want me to be. I accept You now as my Lord and Savior.

Thank You for making me a new person and forgiving my sins, in Jesus' name. Amen.

CONCLUSION

It is my genuine desire that the words in this book empowered, inspired, encouraged, and blessed you in an exceptional way, igniting your prayer life. May you be infused with the love and peace of our God.

Now unto him that is able to keep you from falling, and to present you faultless before the presence of his glory with exceeding joy, to the only wise God our Savior, be glory and majesty, dominion and power, both now and ever. Amen.

I would love to hear and receive your praise reports or testimonies of how this book has been a blessing to you.

You can write to:

Primlavora Humphries
P. O Box 903
Bellwood, Illinois 60104

Visit:
primlavorahumphries.com
Or email me at:
primlavorah@gmail.com

ABOUT THE AUTHOR

Primlavora Humphries was raised in the city of Chicago. She is a licensed and ordained minister, serves as a spiritual adviser and role model. She constantly empowers, encourages, and motivates people to strive to reach their highest potential in life. She uses biblical principles and teaching to inspire others to keep going even when the going seems tough. Primlavora served as boys and girls club instructor, praise and worship president, church librarian and youth director. She currently leads the community prayer service weekly at her church home.

For approximately twelve years, Primlavora worked as a Group Home Coordinator and a Mental Health Professional with a child welfare agency, that provides a structured, nurturing living environment for teenage girls. She currently works as a Behavior Support Specialist, serving children and adults with disabilities to achieve their highest level of independence through quality programs.

Mrs. Humphries is the founder of JusHelp Incorporated, a nonprofit 501c3 organization formed to minister relief, by providing programs designed to empower, inspire and give hope to individuals and families in the midst of life challenges within our communities. Her motto "We Need Each Other."

She currently resides in Bellwood, Illinois with her amazing husband of 27 years Minister James Humphries Sr. They are the proud parents of four adult children James, Sada, Raven and Mason and the grandparents of one beautiful granddaughter Brooklyn.